QUEEN·VICTORIA·AND·HER·PEOPLE·

# Picture book of
# London

ALBERT

D C May

# Picture book of
# London

## Preface by the Earl Grosvenor

**Hamlyn**

London · New York · Sydney · Toronto

Published by
The Hamlyn Publishing Group Limited
London · New York · Sydney · Toronto
Astronaut House, Feltham, Middlesex, England
© The Hamlyn Publishing Group Limited 1977

Reprinted in 1979

ISBN 0 600 37144 1

Printed in Italy
by New Interlitho, Milan

*endpapers*
With the precision of toy
soldiers, a regimental band of
Foot Guards attends the
Trooping of the Colour.
*half-title page*
'Albert the Good' seated in
Kensington Gardens, one of
the most famous public
monuments to Queen Victoria's
husband
*title spread*
The Terrace Front of the
Houses of Parliament.
Whenever Parliament is sitting,
a Union Jack flies from the top
of the great Victoria Tower.
*contents spread*
The White Tower: Norman
architecture at its most
implacable. Oldest of the
towers within the Tower of
London, its walls are 15 feet
thick at the base, 11 feet at
the top.
*preface spread*
As night falls, St Paul's
Cathedral reasserts its
centuries-old domination
over the City of London.

# Contents

# Preface

On leafing through the pages of this book, I am immediately struck by the wealth of historical interest which is encompassed within the bounds of this ageless city.

For myself, I feel privileged to be associated with, and surrounded by, such beauty. We Londoners have an enormous responsibility to our successors to preserve and maintain the high standards set by our forbears, for the benefit not only of ourselves, but for the many thousands of our overseas friends who come to visit London as one of the leading cultural centres of the world. We are enjoying a legacy which has been preserved and handed down to us by past generations. With careful planning, it is possible to combine conservation and a programme of modern development so as to maintain the essential character and beauty of our city while at the same time providing all the necessary modern services and standards. I have always felt that we have never side-stepped our obligations, nor accepted compromise, and this is clearly shown by the superb illustrations in this book.

To achieve such balance is not an easy task in these days when the odds are against us, but as I see it, we are merely caretakers of this jewel in the crown of history. In the past, London has been plagued, burned and bombed, but in the true traditions of this country, she has risen like a phoenix to her former glory. This must be due to the resilience and determination of her citizens and their love for their city.

London holds a fascination for all people and I commend it to you. I am also happy to commend this book because it so adequately transmits the feeling of this great city through its pages.

*Grosvenor*

Earl Grosvenor
Davies Street, London

7

# Introduction

My best time to show London to a newcomer would be on a warm spring morning. When London has the sun on it, the town is transformed, the range of possibilities expands. The sun warms the ground and Londoners respond by politely ambushing each other with agreeable surprises: a long-silent neighbour stops hibernating and speaks; a bus arrives on time, and everyone in the queue says, 'After you'; a traffic warden smiles; a dog wags its tail; a shop front ventures a striped awning; people walk about coatless, for the fun of it. It is as if the Sales have started and the price tags are falling to the floor.

Where should we go, my newcomer and I? Given plenty of time, London is best explored obliquely. The two-day visitor may have to dash round the principal sights or miss seeing them entirely; but the visitor with two weeks to spare, or more, can afford to take London as it comes, the way Londoners do; that way lies a far deeper relationship. As for the method, it is very simple: take a district, not too large, and walk around it, letting the famous sights and the small ones commingle, and watching Londoners lead their lives.

In Chelsea, for instance, set out from Sloane Square by the Royal Court Theatre and saunter along the King's Road, looking at the shops. Turn left into the broad walk of Royal Avenue and walk down the middle, around Burton Court to Wren's Royal Hospital, where the Chelsea Pensioners live. Explore the Hospital as you will, then continue to the Embankment via Tite Street, where at various times J. S. Sargent, Oscar Wilde and James McNeill Whistler lived. On the Embankment, walk past the Apothecaries' Physic Garden and cross over to the river wall to see the Thames. On the far bank is Battersea Park, lit up at night, the painted Chelsea Bridge behind. Walk past Albert Bridge to Cheyne Walk and up Cheyne Row to Carlyle's House, the home of the nineteenth-century historian, sometimes called the 'Sage of Chelsea'. The house is now a National Trust property and visitors may see its small rooms preserved as they were lived in by the Carlyles: in the basement kitchen Carlyle and Tennyson talked and smoked together; in the attic study Carlyle, an insomniac, built double walls in a vain search for peace and quiet. Leaving the house, carry on down the Embankment, all the while looking out for blue plaques on house walls commemorating the famous who lived in them, past Chelsea Old Church and Crosby Hall to Battersea Bridge. In Beaufort Street catch a No. 19 bus back to Sloane Square – or go on to Knightsbridge, thence to Kensington or the West End. Always, the system is: cover a smallish area at leisure, break for refreshments or a meal, and move on.

London is too big to rush. A city some forty miles wide, as high as the Post Office Tower and as deep as the platforms on Goodge Street Tube Station near by, is obviously a place of many levels, a jumble of strange juxtapositions. So its history proves. Founded by the Romans, fortified by William the Conqueror, greatly expanded by the Tudor kings and queens, destroyed by the Great Fire of 1666, rebuilt by Wren and the architects of Charles II and William and Mary, further enlarged under the Georges and Queen Victoria, bombed by the Nazis, again rebuilt, this time with concrete and glass . . . expansion continually following destruction, London's evolution has been going on for two thousand years. And over the last two hundred, the town and its suburbs have mushroomed. In 1779 *Boswell's Johnson* offered the notion that 'The chief advantage of London is, that a man is always so near his burrow.' Today, as we emerge from bus and Tube with aching ribs and boil with rage in traffic jams, it is hard to believe that it was ever so.

Today's Londoners must bustle urgently about, travelling many miles between burrow and place of work or school, battling home with the shopping. In the course of this change of habitat and the speeding up of their mode of life, Londoners have developed some rituals that a newcomer, arriving in their midst, may find baffling. For their amusement and edification (though Londoners too may test its assertions), we have assembled a summary of a typical London week. The guiding principle is that each day is different because different things happen to change the mood, setting Friday apart from Thursday, for example, and Thursday from Wednesday.

*Welcome, then, to Londoners' London.*
The focal point of the London week is Saturday, or, more precisely, Saturday night. However, to avoid inducing at a too early stage either the Sunday-morning blues or the all-Monday blacks, we begin with Thursday. The suggested menus are typical of what the inhabitants eat and versions may be found in steamy cafés, pubs or a friend's house that are quite as good as those served in hotels and carpeted eating houses. Their position in the week is fairly arbitrary but does sometimes reflect the mood of the day and the likely state of a Londoner's pocket or purse at that juncture of the week.

*Thursday*
A traditional payday. The week, from its halfway sag, is beginning to pick itself up, ready for the run-in to Saturday night. An early closing day (13.00 usually) for shops in certain districts. With matching illogic, it's the week's late shopping night in West End stores (open until 19.00 or later). Your London menu: try Steak and kidney pie, followed by Baked jam roll and custard.

*Friday*
Also known as 'good old Friday', its advent celebrated by

extensive lunching. Pubs may be hard to get into: apply extra force when pushing on bar doors. Day of the big domestic shopping expedition: in residential districts, especially, beware being run down by loaded supermarket trolleys or tripped by empty ones, sometimes hard to detect on dimly lit pavements. Not a good day to have your hair done (unless you have booked weeks ahead or have a hold over your coiffeur). The homeward rush of the office workers begins early today: from 15.30 public transport can be unsuitable for claustrophobes. Dish of the day: Prawn sandwiches and Draught Guinness.

## Saturday

The high-day of the playful Londoner. Children kick off with early-morning cinema shows (Laurel & Hardy, SF, Bugs Bunny, etc.), and adults follow up by getting married (11.00–15.00 are most-favoured times). In the football season the well-known British sense of fair play is parodied at various League stadiums by youthful groups with fanciful names like 'QPR Boot Boys' and 'Shed' (their aerosol graffiti much in evidence on the Underground). Another bad day at the hairdressers, unless they know you: from Dalston to Camberwell maidens parade in curlers and chiffon scarves (they did it their way). Night falls and the four-wheeled chariots move Up-West, to the lights, fights and festivals of W.1. Away from this principal hub, bingo halls dispense large cash prizes. Everywhere, theatres, cinemas and pubs have their biggest night. Afterwards the streets slowly empty, leaving just a scattering of people who had said, 'Let's go on somewhere', and then couldn't find it. Eat at a jellied eel stall, as found at Aldgate East (Tubby Isaacs), or buy a pot beforehand in Harrod's Food Hall, Soho or Fortnum & Mason; the contents are best consumed outdoors – nobody will thank you for eating them on the last bus home. If up all night, the Cavendish Hotel, Jermyn Street, serves breakfast round the clock.

## Sunday

A slow-waking day, interrupted by the dong of church bells. Few shops are open other than newsagents and tobacconists except in the main tourist areas. By mid-morning, Londoners are busy with traditional activities: park football, granny visiting, car washing. If fine, try a walk by the river, at Hammersmith, say, or Kew; or tackle a street market – East Street, off the Walworth Road, or 'Petticoat Lane' (Middlesex Street). Pub hours are scarcely better than in those outer limbs of the United Kingdom where they don't open at all: 12.00–14.00 and 19.00–22.30. Afternoons are for listening to outraged opinion (Speakers' Corner) and contemplating statues (across the grass in Hyde Park and Kensington Gardens). Eventually the cinemas open. Evenings are a much-muted

form of Saturday night. Lunch, sometimes called Dinner, must include at least one of: Roast beef and Yorkshire pudding, Roast lamb and mint sauce, Roast pork and apple sauce.

## Monday

The growing popularity of the long weekend has made some shopkeepers disinclined to open today. Don't fight it, go window shopping instead. Reflect on your own weekend over an English tea, say at the Ritz, Brown's Hotel or the Savoy, or in one of the big stores. Glean notepaper and write someone a letter. Your dishes today: Shepherd's pie; Prunes and custard.

## Tuesday

In a land of slow-starters it is not surprising to find that some natives of the capital think the week starts here. See them, sleep-haunted, hurrying, stumbling, everywhere and nowhere. Not a day of inherently strong mood: in season, try a cricket match, at Lord's or the Oval; take a trip on the river; seek out one of the smaller parks, or Kew Gardens; go to a museum – those in London are many and varied, so check them in a newspaper first. The food: English cheeses, chutney, pickles.

## Wednesday

Early closing day (13.00 usually) in some districts; but late-night shopping in Knightsbridge. Wednesdays can be a low point. Many people agree on this. Shopkeepers so disposed may be less than charming when asked for goods not easily accessible, i.e. not on the shelf beside them. This feeling can adversely affect bus-conductors (passengers brusquely forbidden to sit on each other's laps), Tube guards (mind your fingers), taxi drivers (they suddenly go off duty), ladies of the night ('Too early for me, dear'). A big night, none the less, for organized sports such as football, greyhound racing, ice hockey, etc. Also, regressing somewhat, a traditional afternoon for theatre matinees (for these and the sporting fixtures, see the daily newspapers). Your food today: Fish and chips.

*And so to . . . Thursday.*

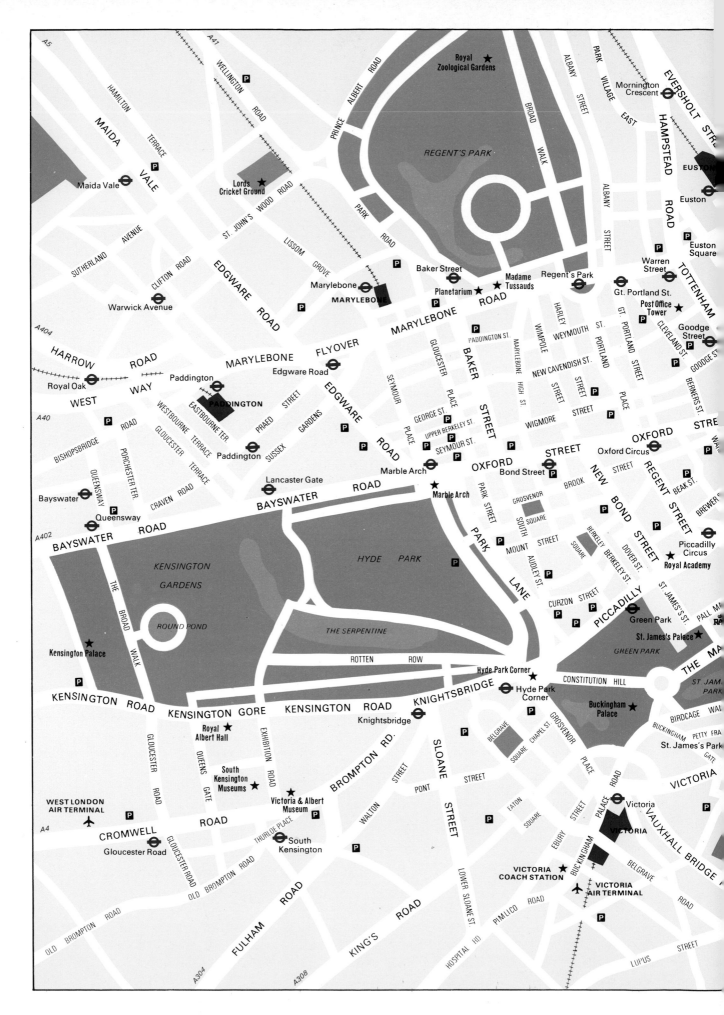

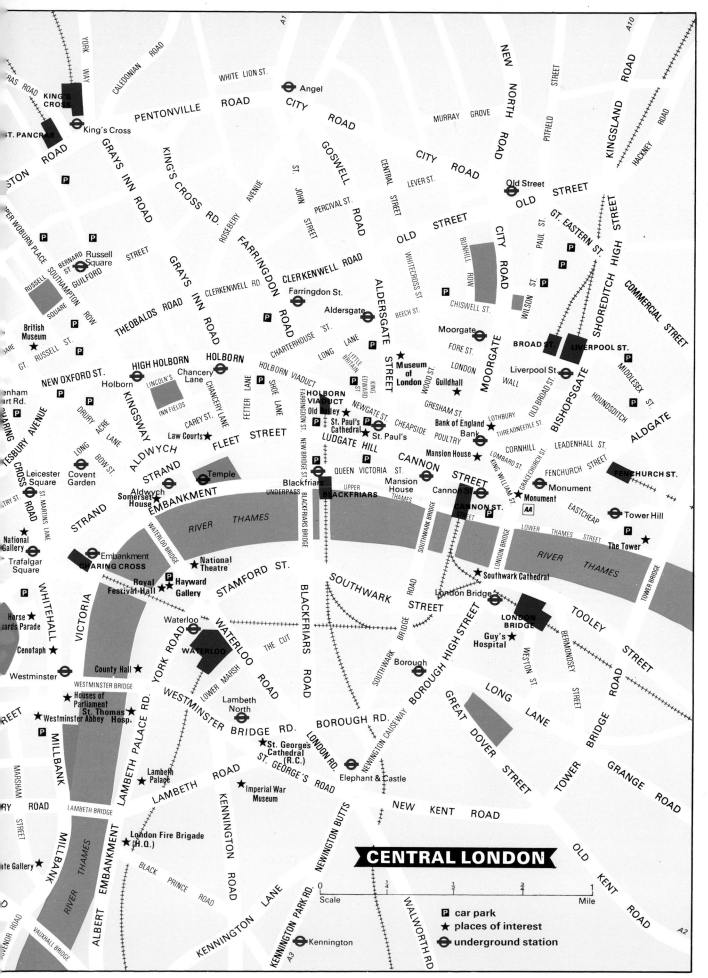

**CENTRAL LONDON**

Scale
0   ¼   ½   ¾   1
Mile

🅿 car park
★ places of interest
Ⓤ underground station

© John Bartholomew & Son Limited

Buckingham Palace, principal
residence of the English monarch.
The Palace is a surprisingly recent
creation: originally a country
mansion called Buckingham
House, its conversion into a palace
began in the 1820s when John
Nash drew up plans later
modified by other hands. The
front, seen here, dates from 1913
and is by Sir Aston Webb, who
also conceived the massive
Victoria Memorial in front of the
Palace; this features the Queen in
white marble watched over by a
gilt Victory.

# First Sightings

Even a flying visitor, propelled around town by an itinerary that left him or her with the option of 'doing' London against the clock or not at all, may still expect, by careful selection, to see enough in two or three days to compensate for such temporary discomforts as hot feet or cultural dazzle. The barest minimum would be to see the five places given extended descriptions in this chapter: Westminster Abbey, the Houses of Parliament, St Paul's Cathedral, the Tower of London and Greenwich. Respectively the national shrine, the seat of government, the most celebrated church, the most celebrated fortress and the finest architectural complex, they are probably London's greatest treasures. In going to see them, moreover, the visitor would also have a chance to look at the Thames and Dockland (beside the Tower and on the way to Greenwich); he would observe and travel along the great thoroughfares of Whitehall, the Strand and Fleet Street (while going to St Paul's); a brief detour would take in the West End – Piccadilly, Leicester Square, a flash of Soho – and he would cross the City en route for the Tower.

Although Greater London covers a vast acreage, the principal places of interest are for the most part to be found in adjacent central districts. Working eastwards from Chelsea or Kensington, one soon comes to the heart of it all: in essence, a long gourd-shape of streets, squares and gardens, its boundary running east along Oxford Street to Holborn, the City and the Tower, then back beside the river to Westminster and Chelsea, and so round to Hyde Park. Not only the home of the great palaces, cathedrals and central parks, its other attractions include London's most elegant shops, in Bond Street, Piccadilly and the arcades and streets near by; the gentle world of clubland is centred on St James's, where the capital's élite ritually snooze beneath bulky newspapers; around St Martin's Lane and Shaftesbury Avenue are the theatres, the world's finest; to the north-east of Piccadilly Circus is the square mile of Soho, the dark lady of London; while

13

to the east, around the Strand and Fleet Street, are the centres of London's judicial system and its newspapers, and still farther east the financial heart, in the City of London.

Among such grandeur, mile upon mile, the visitor may feel overcome with an Awful Plenitude. How is it possible to absorb, in a few days, even weeks, such a rich diet of architecture, history and custom? Always, though, the story of a building is a composite of the deeds of individuals – real or legendary. Usually it is possible to discover some human factor which symbolizes or illuminates the grand design. An example, in Westminster Abbey, is the Tomb of the Unknown Warrior: beneath the pavement in the nave lies a nameless corpse brought home from Flanders after World War I; buried beside kings and famous men, it is his presence that most movingly explains the Abbey's function as a shrine of remembrance.

opposite, above
One of the four faces of Big Ben, the nation's timepiece, seen from behind the Boadicea statue on the Embankment. The great Clock Tower of the Houses of Parliament takes its name from Sir Benjamin Hall, Commissioner of Works when the bell was hung, in 1858.

opposite, below
Number Ten Downing Street, the house in which the Prime Minister lives. Only four houses remain of the original Downing Street, a modest cul-de-sac built in about 1680; steps leading from the end of the street down to St James's Park were added at a later date. Number Ten is the heart of a governmental complex far larger than would seem possible, to judge from the exterior alone: internal passages link it to its neighbours in Downing Street and to a much larger house at the back. There is also a charming walled garden.

below
A summertime crowd on the steps of the Eros statue in Piccadilly Circus . . . islanders of many races happy to pass the day among each other's paper bags and chocolate wrappers, watching the buses come and go.

# Westminster Abbey

At one time a Benedictine monastery standing on an island beside a ford across the Thames, the Abbey in its thousand-year history has survived and even been enhanced by the ceaseless attentions of builders, masons, architects and their royal patrons. In its present, highly encrusted state it has achieved the peculiar rank of a national shrine. The old abbey church, partly rebuilt by Edward the Confessor a century after the monastery's foundation in 960, has swelled into the lofty and magnificent building where the kings and queens of England are crowned, where royal marriages are consecrated and memorial services held to honour great servants of the nation.

The Abbey's high nave and indeed its over-all character reflect a French Gothic influence, drawn mainly from the Cathedral of Rheims. Around this dominant scheme almost every architectural period has a presence: Saxon and Norman, Early English, Decorated and Perpendicular, through to the eighteenth-century western towers, designed by Hawksmoor, and the nineteenth-century Gothic of Sir George Gilbert Scott's north transept. As befits a national shrine, the Abbey is also superlatively rich in chapels and monuments. There is the gigantic tomb of Edward the Confessor, and monuments to Henry III and many later English kings and queens; even grander in its isolation is Henry VII's magnificent chapel at the extreme eastern end. Among the Abbey's other treasures are the oak Coronation Chair of Edward I and the memorials in Poets' Corner, where many of England's great literary men are buried.

Outside the church the Abbey precincts embrace the medieval cloisters begun by Henry III in about 1245; the Dean's residence and garden, formerly that of the abbot; the Refectory, the Chapter House, and the Pyx Chapel and Museum. In the latter are housed fully dressed wax figures of Elizabeth I, Charles II, Lord Nelson, William Pitt and many others who were given a State funeral. These 'waxworks' were originally made to be placed beside the grave or monument, and provided a lifelike image of the dead person while his or her memorial sculpture was being prepared.

*The Abbey from Dean's Yard.
From this south-westerly
viewpoint, the dominant features
are the two western towers, the
flying buttresses along the nave and
the spiky turrets of the Chapter
House.*

*The nave, whose proportions are akin to the tall, narrow thirteenth-century cathedrals at Rheims and Amiens, and whose vault is the highest Gothic vault in England, rising to 102 feet. The vaulting is carried on distinctive dark piers of Purbeck marble.*

**left**

*Poets' Corner, in the south transept. This part of the Abbey contains monuments to Chaucer, Ben Jonson, Shakespeare, Spenser, Milton, Browning, Tennyson, Dickens, Hardy and a score of other eminent literary men.*

**below left**

*The gilded bronze effigy of Eleanor of Castile, wife of Edward I; her tomb is protected on one side by a decorative iron grille made in 1294 by Thomas de Leighton.*

**below**

*Edward I's Coronation Chair, made in 1300 and enclosing the Stone of Scone, on which a long line of Scottish kings was crowned. Edward captured the stone in 1297 and for almost seven hundred years English kings and queens have been crowned on this chair.*

below
*The view south along Cumberland Terrace, one of Nash's sparkling stucco terraces that face Regent's Park. In front of the houses, which date from about 1827, stand cast-iron gas lamps, elegant emblems of an earlier industrial age.*

opposite, above
*Mellow lighting and gracious symmetry in John Nash's Royal Opera Arcade, off Pall Mall. This was London's first arcade, inspired by Parisian examples; the bow-fronted shops run north to Charles II Street.*

opposite, below
*The Royal Albert Hall, from the steps on the south side. This huge amphitheatre, notorious for its acoustic problems, was built in memory of Queen Victoria's Consort and stages a range of events that defies cultural bracketing: anything from a wrestling match to a promenade concert.*

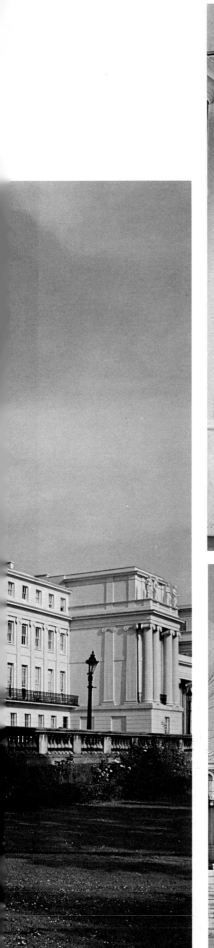

# The Houses of Parliament

The present buildings, by the Gothicists Charles Barry and Augustus Pugin, occupy the site of the old Palace of Westminster, which was consumed by fire in 1834. A competition was held to determine who should provide the nation with its new seat of government. First prize went to Barry, who then called in the dynamic, temperamental Pugin to help him. Together they developed a solution based on one long building that would contain the two main Chambers – the House of Lords for the peers and the House of Commons for the commoners, together with their lobbies, a Prince's Chamber, a Royal Gallery and a multitude of supplementary rooms. Pugin, possibly the most inventive of Victorian Gothic architects, applied his talents chiefly to the ornamentation of Barry's master scheme, designing details of wood and metalwork down to the last inkstand and coat-hanger. In his designs for the House of Lords, it is generally agreed, Pugin surpassed himself. Working with a sombre colour scheme of golds and browns, the red leather seats making an almost brilliant contrast, Pugin created a superbly detailed room dominated by a canopied throne flanked by brass candelabra, the walls decorated with frescoes and statues of the Magna Carta barons.

The House of Commons is less exuberant. The nineteenth-century Chamber was destroyed by bombing in World War II and was then rebuilt in the Gothic style – but in an austere age a century after the volatile Pugin this was not, perhaps, the best decision. It is more rewarding to turn to the exterior, there to admire Barry's three great towers. To the east is the Clock Tower of Big Ben, the astonishing profusion of its upper details drawn from Flemish Gothic models. To the west, taller and more massive by far, is the Victoria Tower, rising 400 feet to the top of its flagstaff; at its foot is the Royal Entrance to Parliament. In between the two is the 300-foot Middle Tower, its spired lantern crowning the Central Lobby.

*The Chamber of the House of Lords, Pugin's masterpiece. In World War II a bomb crashed through the roof of the Chamber, split one of the front benches and buried itself in the floor, but did not explode.*

**right**
*The Chamber of the House of Commons, rebuilt in a muted Gothic style after World War II. Between the two sets of benches is the Speaker's chair; Members of the Government sit on his right, the Opposition on his left.*

**below right**
*The ornate ceiling of the Central Lobby, an octagonal structure decorated with sculpture and floral motifs. The vaulting forms a star around the centre of the ceiling. When Parliament is in session, visitors wishing to see members are admitted to the Central Lobby. Policemen on duty in the hall then contact the appropriate member.*

**opposite**
*The long sweep of the riverside terrace, where Members of Parliament customarily entertain their guests to tea. Behind the visitors soar the buttresses and pinnacles of Barry's façade.*

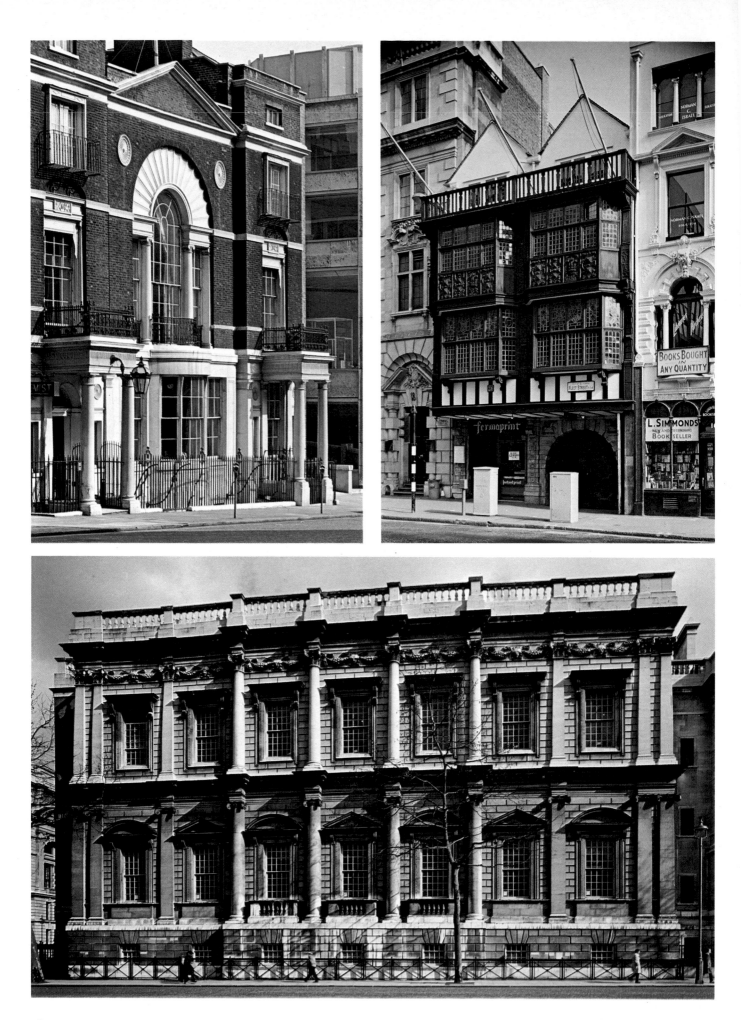

*opposite, above left*
*Boodle's Club in St James's*
*Street, designed in 1775 by John*
*Crunden. Beside it is part of* The
Economist *building, completed*
*in 1964, one of London's more*
*successful modern office buildings.*

*opposite, above right*
*Number Seventeen Fleet Street, a*
*fine timbered house with projecting*
*upper storeys that dates from*
*1610. The house contains Prince*
*Henry's Room, which has a*
*decorated ceiling and is named*
*after the elder son of James I.*
*Through the arch is a passageway*
*leading to the twelfth-century*
*Temple Church.*

*opposite, below*
*The Banqueting House in*
*Whitehall, designed by Inigo Jones*
*in 1619; its severe Palladian style*
*was both a revelation and a source*
*of acrimonious dispute among*
*Londoners of the day.*

*below*
*The view down the slope of St*
*James's Street to the turreted*
*gatehouse of St James's Palace,*
*built by Henry VIII on the site of*
*a hospital for 'leprous maidens'.*

# St Paul's Cathedral

Fires destroyed two churches on the site of St Paul's before construction began in 1675 of the present cathedral, London's most famous church and Sir Christopher Wren's masterpiece. Whether a Roman temple of Diana also once stood there has not been firmly established. What is certain is that a seventh-century Christian church was burned down in 1087, to be succeeded by the Norman church of Old St Paul's. Sections of this building were lost at various times – probably the most spectacular departure being that of the steeple, destroyed by lightning in 1561 – before the Great Fire of London in 1666 brought down virtually the whole cathedral.

After twenty-two years of patient building, the first service in Wren's new cathedral was held in 1697, the last stone being laid eleven years after that. During the final phase, the erection of the dome and lantern, the architect, then an old man, was hauled up in a basket once a week to inspect progress. The ultimate glory of St Paul's is its graceful lead-coated dome,

crowned by the lantern, ball and cross. The dome is 112 feet in diameter, and from the top of the cross it is 365 feet to the cathedral pavement.

The plan of the building is that of the traditional long cross: its structure combines baroque and classical elements in a restrained 'English' style that is a principal distinguishing mark of Wren and his contemporaries. From the west the visitor passes up the steps and through the lower of two colonnades, there to be confronted by the long nave, augustly beautiful, leading to the domed crossing – the interior of the great drum on which the dome rests. The cool monumental character of the interior is sustained by many a tomb and memorial sculpture, in particular to heroes of the Napoleonic Wars. Warmer in atmosphere are the superbly carved choir stalls of Grinling Gibbons; admirers of fine craftsmanship will also remember the wrought-iron gates by Jean Tijou which separate the High Altar from the choir aisles.

right

*Looking into the dome. Above the windows are eight frescoes by Sir James Thornhill depicting the life of St Paul; beyond these, no more than thimble-size in the photograph, is the lantern, surmounted in turn by the famous cross. Below the windows is the Whispering Gallery. Make a sound, however softly, up there and it will be reflected off the dome and heard over a considerable distance.*

opposite

*The west façade, from the top of Ludgate Hill. In front stands a statue of Queen Anne, during whose reign the building was completed (in 1708). In the left-hand tower is a peal of bells, in the right the clock and Great Paul, a massive bell rung once a day.*

opposite, above
*The turrets, pinnacles and pointed arches of the Royal Courts of Justice. This monument to Victorian Gothic architecture lies at the eastern extremity of the Strand and is the creation of George Street. In the middle of the road, opposite the far corner of the Royal Courts, stands the Temple Bar Memorial, marking the entrance to the City of London.*

opposite, below left
*Trees in leaf in Middle Temple Lane, which runs south from Temple Bar to the Thames Embankment.*

opposite, below right
*King's Bench Walk, also in the Temple – the legal enclave that occupies a discreet rectangle between Fleet Street and the Thames. This is the home of two Inns of Court, the Inner and Middle Temples.*

below
*The Lady Chapel in Westminster Cathedral, rich in mosaics. The Cathedral is the principal Roman Catholic church in England, and is situated near the lower end of Victoria Street. It was designed in the 1890s by J. F. Bentley in a neo-Byzantine style.*

# The Tower of London

The stone turrets and high battlements of William the Conqueror's White Tower, opposite, served for centuries as a model prison-cum-stronghold. Their grandeur testifies to the insecurity of despotic monarchs: in those days when the notion of democracy was something that even philosophers hesitated to tell their best friends about, the Tower – if he or she lived that long – was the regular destination of anyone questioning the might of the throne or the wisdom of whoever was sitting on it at the time.

The White Tower is the citadel of a complex that grew up around it as later monarchs sought to make it still more secure. In time it was enclosed by an inner curtain wall with twelve bastion towers, a moat and an outer wall. Although the Tower was primarily conceived as a military installation to guard the eastern approaches to London, its career as a place of incarceration for State prisoners was certainly under way by 1305, when Sir William Wallace, the Scottish insurgent, was executed there by the gruesome method of hanging, drawing and quartering. The last person to be beheaded in England, Lord Lovat, suffered his fate at the Tower in 1747. Between those two dates, a long line of monarchs, their wives, ambitious courtiers, prisoners of war and traitors spent miserable years there awaiting release of one kind or another. Since then, too, numerous State prisoners have been kept in the Tower, the latest being Rudolf Hess, the Nazi who escaped to England in World War II.

The Tower has also served as a royal residence, a mint and a menagerie; the ravens are the sole survivors of the latter, which was incorporated with the Regent's Park Zoo in 1834. Two other important collections are still to be seen there: the Crown Jewels, including the Imperial State Crown and the Jewelled Sword of State, and the Armouries, founded by Henry VIII and displaying many fine examples of equestrian armour, early mortars and cannon.

opposite
*Traitors' Gate, now separated from the river, once the way in for hapless prisoners. Few escaped.*

left
*Tower Green, with the Queen's House at the far end, adjoining the Yeoman Gaoler's House, in which Lady Jane Grey was imprisoned. In the foreground is the old execution block.*

below
*The White Tower, the centre of the fortress, seen from Tower Bridge.*

*The financier's recipe for a
trustworthy image – a façade of
tall columns surmounted by a
weighty pediment – as seen in
triplicate at Bank, the triangular-
shaped junction in the heart of the
City. First, above left, the
Bank of England, the
Government's bank, rebuilt in
1921–37 by Sir Herbert Baker*

*with a heavy portico of paired
columns rising within the outer
wall of Sir John Soane's earlier
eighteenth-century building. In the
pediment is the 'Old Lady of
Threadneedle Street'. Second,
above right, the Royal
Exchange. Standing at right
angles to the Bank of England, the
building dates from the 1840s.
Two previous Exchanges were*

*burned down; it is now the head
office of an insurance company.
Third, below, the Mansion
House, best of the three buildings
and the official residence of the
Lord Mayor of London. The
Corinthian portico, completed in
1753, is by George Dance the
Elder. Inside the building,
mayoral banquets are held in the
Egyptian Hall.*

*Guildhall, dating in part from
1411–35: scene of the Lord
Mayor's election and Corporation
state banquets.*

# Greenwich

Six and a half miles down river from Westminster Bridge is Greenwich, an old and architecturally distinguished town-suburb with many pleasant Georgian terraces and a fine park laid out in the 1660s under the direction of Charles II. At that time Greenwich and its neighbour, Deptford, where the Royal Naval construction yards were situated, formed an important maritime centre. Ships of the East India Company's fleet were built there and Samuel Pepys, today more famous for his perceptive and marvellously indiscreet diary, was for several years Secretary of the Admiralty and spent many hours in Greenwich supervising the works. A fitting memorial to the age of sail stands by the waterside: the *Cutty Sark,* a great three-masted tea clipper, which stands in dry dock, restored and containing a small museum of ships' figureheads.

Greatest of all Greenwich's treasures, however, is the superb extended quadrangle of buildings that now fulfils the dual function of housing the Royal Naval College and the National Maritime Museum. This is the Royal Hospital, as conceived by Sir Christopher Wren. The buildings bear the stylistic influences of other great architects, in particular Hawksmoor and Vanbrugh, who collaborated with Wren, and Inigo Jones, who planned the earlier waterside house, King Charles's Block, and the Queen's House, both of which Wren incorporated in his scheme. The Royal Hospital was founded for the benefit of wounded and exhausted seamen, similar in its aims to the Royal Hospital in Chelsea for army 'Pensioners'. It remained a naval hospital until 1873, and was then converted into a college for the training of naval officers.

Behind Wren's Royal Hospital rise the slopes of Greenwich Park where stands the Observatory, now a museum of astronomy and navigation. Here Sir John Flamsteed compiled a famous star catalogue which was to equip mariners with a dependable means of calculating longitude at sea. Greenwich was then adopted as the standard meridian, positions being expressed in degrees or time east or west of it; hence the establishment of Greenwich Mean Time, the system by which worldwide time may be calculated.

*Wren's grand scheme for the Royal Hospital. At the water's edge are Queen Anne's House, to the left, and King Charles's Block to the right. Behind them, and forming the far corners of a great court are the domed Queen Mary and King William Blocks; in the distance is the Queen's House, with the Observatory just visible on the hill to the rear. The Queen's House is now the National Maritime Museum and the buildings nearer the river form the Royal Naval College.*

above
*The Observatory in Greenwich Park, founded in 1675 for Sir John Flamsteed, first Astronomer Royal. On the path in front of the Observatory is marked the zero meridian of longitude, which passes through Greenwich.*

right
*The Tulip Staircase in the Queen's House.*

opposite
*The Painted Hall, formerly the Hospital dining-room, in what is now the Royal Naval College. The ceiling paintings are by Sir James Thornhill.*

above
*Feeding some of Trafalgar Square's huge population of scruffy but generally amiable pigeons.*

above right
*Above it all . . . Lord Nelson, the hero of the Battle of Trafalgar (1805), looks out from the top of his Column.*

right
*The spired eighteenth-century Church of St Martin-in-the-Fields, seen from beside one of the fountains of Trafalgar Square.*

opposite, above
*Admiralty Arch, designed by Sir Aston Webb as a memorial to Queen Victoria; this triumphal arch leads to the Mall, St James's Park and, at the far end, Buckingham Palace.*

opposite, below
*The National Gallery, not as imposing as it might have been given its raised site along the north side of Trafalgar Square, but entirely successful as a museum, housing a remarkable collection of paintings.*

*Guardsmen march beside the lake in St James's Park. Linking Buckingham Palace to Horse Guards Parade and Whitehall – the monarch to the means of government – St James's Park* *has royal associations extending back to Henry VIII, who first enclosed it. The present park was designed in 1827 by John Nash for George IV.*

# The Royal Parks

Viewed on the map, London's central parks –
patches of green enclosed by a more sombre maze
representing streets and railway lines – may seem to
occupy an unexpectedly large spread. Two principal
shapes, erratic in their geometry, command the
attention. To the north is the near-circle of Regent's
Park, surmounted by the curve of Primrose Hill.
Lower down and slightly to the west is the great
oblong of Kensington Gardens-Hyde Park, almost
bisected by the Serpentine and flanked on its south-
eastern edge by a smaller, irregular, winged figure
composed of Green Park, St James's Park and the
Queen's private park – the grounds of Buckingham
Palace.

All these rich expanses belong to the Crown. All,
with the exception of the gardens of Buckingham
Palace, are open to everyone. They form the nucleus
of London's royal parks. And they *are* large. From
Notting Hill to Trafalgar Square is at least a three-
mile walk and yet, allowing for just two road
crossings and a short stretch of pavement at the
finish, the journey can be made entirely through
parkland: over the wooded rides and grassy acres of
Hyde Park, down the gentle slopes of Green Park
and along the more intimate pathways of St James's
Park, the latter abundant with flowers, ducks, geese
and, oddly enough, pelicans. Such compelling
creatures cannot be there except by design: they are,
indeed, part of a tradition, begun by Charles II
(reigned 1660–85), who introduced to the park
'severall sorts of ordinary and extraordinary wild
fowle', as the diarist John Evelyn recorded.

If one ruler of England were to be chosen as the
true begetter of London's royal parks, that person
would be Charles II. Before him, in the sixteenth
century, Henry VIII and Elizabeth I had encouraged
hunting, tournaments and outdoor pageants in the
vicinity of their palaces. It remained to Charles II to
give civilized shape to these still partly wild fields
and woodlands. He redesigned St James's Park in
the French style, bought Green Park and took his
constitutionals there (whence the origin, it is

thought, of the name Constitution Hill). Farther afield he developed Richmond Park, created for hunting in 1637 by his father, Charles I, and himself instigated the laying out of Greenwich Park. At Hampton Court, earlier the royal palace of Henry VIII, he contributed the French-style Long Water. Very likely, too, he cast an eye over near-by Bushy Park, last of the ten royal parks, where soon after his death Sir Christopher Wren designed a grand Chestnut Avenue.

The royal parks make a random pattern on the face of Greater London. Surrounding them is a denser network of commons, squares and gardens – not all so arrestingly designed but treasured by the many who use them. From the vales and thickets of Hampstead Heath in the north to the compact slopes of One Tree Hill, Honor Oak, which offers grand vistas over the city from its southernmost edge, all express something of the Londoner's cautious regard for the Great Outdoors.

opposite
*Winter sunlight pierces a group of trees in St James's Park. All here is calm, but only a few steps away through the mist stand the towers and turrets of Westminster, where buildings are encircled by an endless noisy caravan of cars, lorries, buses and taxis.*

above
*Fallow deer from the Queen's herd graze in Richmond Park. There are, more precisely, two royal herds — one of some 250 large red deer and another of about 350 dappled fallow deer — which roam freely over the park's 2,400 acres.*

left
*Ornamental gates beside Green Park, an undulating, tree-shaded expanse between Piccadilly and Constitution Hill, once favoured as a duelling ground by noblemen anxious for their honour.*

above
*Fountains on the Long Water in Kensington Gardens. Indifferent to ice and snow, the maiden's water pot flows on, unwaveringly splashing one of the four mermaids who form the centrepiece – a fountain that plays into a shallow fluted basin.*

opposite
*Springtime in Kensington Gardens: at the end of an avenue of trees sits the bronze effigy of Prince Albert, Queen Victoria's much-mourned Consort. He sits beneath a huge pointed canopy, holding a catalogue of the Great*

*Exhibition of 1851 and looking across to the concert hall that also bears his name.*

right
*The bronze Peter Pan statue in Kensington Gardens, made by Sir George Frampton to commemorate Sir James Barrie's boy-who-would-not-grow-up.*

opposite
*An unusual view of the Post Office Tower, taken from beside the boating lake in Regent's Park. The lake, created by John Nash, incorporates several small islands and is also a bird sanctuary, the home of many rare varieties of wildfowl.*

above
*Biggest attraction in Regent's Park Zoo is the Monkey House, where Guy the gorilla – King Kong in three dimensions – was for many years by far the most popular resident. Guy, seen here in a reflective pose, was a star.*

Mellow notes of wind and brass
issue from the octagonal bandstand
in Hyde Park, above; at
Speakers' Corner, opposite, it is
Sunday afternoon and the air is
loud with human cries appropriate
to the wilder shores of oratory.
Here democratic man relishes his
freedom to fly spiritual kites of
every improbable shape and size
before a traditionally disrespectful
audience. 'The End Is At Hand',
claims the banner in our picture;
but the man standing in front of
it, with two fingers raised,
appears to hold other views.

The combined march-past of the
five regiments of the Foot Guards
at the annual Trooping the Colour
ceremony, held on Horse Guards
Parade in honour of the Queen's
official birthday.

# Pageantry and Ceremony

In this chapter we look, principally, at seven ceremonies that are regularly enacted in London. That they are spectacular is beyond question: their purpose, after all, is to assert some power or tradition by a suitable display, colourful enough to be memorable, aggressive enough to carry authority and deter would-be usurpers. Every generation understands these principles. In the eyes of medieval kings and twentieth-century tourists and television audiences alike, there are two essentials to a successful display: noise and swagger. Trumpets, fifes and drums must blast, squeal and thunder. Best uniforms are worn; the gilded coach is finely burnished to its last rococo protuberance, then wheeled out behind six shampooed horses, ornately harnessed and blinkered in black and gold; cannon are unlimbered in the park and roar their allegiance to the Crown; old soldiers parade more passively in remembrance of their founder, a seventeenth-century king.

These assertions of power and continuing privilege are nearly all carried out by the military. The British Redcoat of the Guards Division and his mounted comrades of the Household Cavalry and the Horse Artillery are the stars of the show. They it is who take the lion's share of mounting the permanent guard at Buckingham Palace and the Horse Guards in Whitehall; who troop the Queen's Colour on her birthday, and fire special salutes in her honour. They are to be found at Windsor Castle, too, at such ceremonies as the investiture of new Knights of the Order of the Garter. One further military unit must be mentioned: the Honourable Artillery Company. This is organized in Artillery and Infantry Divisions, which respectively fire salutes at the Tower of London and provide Guards of Honour in the City. Veteran members of the Company belong to the Company of Pikemen and Musketeers; they wear seventeenth-century uniforms and, for example, escort the Lord Mayor's coach on the day of his annual Show.

No less splendid is the permanent pageant

provided by the Yeomen Warders of the Tower. These men, the 'Beefeaters', are selected from retired Army personnel and, like the first Yeomen, a bodyguard formed in 1485 to protect Henry VII, they wear the red and gold Tudor uniform and carry partisans (pikes). A ruff was added to this uniform by Elizabeth I (see the Yeoman on page 56); then in 1858 Queen Victoria introduced a dark blue and red undress uniform, so giving the Yeomen a more workmanlike but still colourful version for everyday wear (this uniform is worn by the Raven Master on page 57). On State occasions the Chief Warder carries a mace, and the Yeoman Gaoler a ceremonial axe. The best-known custom involving the Yeoman Warders is the nightly Ceremony of the Keys, described on pages 56–57, which commemorates the Tower's one-time significance as a stronghold, and underlines its present role as the museum housing the priceless Crown Jewels. It is an instance, typical of many in London, of the present still tightly enmeshed with the past.

above
*A gun crew of the King's Troop, Royal Horse Artillery, fires a ceremonial salute in Hyde Park. Salutes are fired to mark special occasions such as the Queen's birthday or the Opening of Parliament.*

above
*A parade on Oak Apple Day
(29 May) of Chelsea 'Pensioners',
the retired and disabled soldiers
who live at the Royal Hospital.
This parade is held each year on
the anniversary of the entry into
London in 1660 of Charles II,
who founded the Hospital. The
building was designed by Sir
Christopher Wren.*

left
*A veteran of the Hospital watches
the parade. On Oak Apple Day
they exchange their dark blue
winter coats for scarlet ones.*

# Ceremonies at the Tower

Each night at 22.00 the Tower of London is made secure by means of a 600-year-old ritual called the Ceremony of the Keys. The Chief Warder, wearing a Tudor bonnet and scarlet coat, marches with a rifle-armed guard to lock first the outer gate, and then the gates of the Middle Tower and the Byward Tower, both of which are on the perimeter. The Warder's party marches back to the Bloody Tower, where a sentry challenges them with the words, 'Halt! Who goes there?' The exchange then runs its historic course, as follows:

'The keys.'
'Whose keys?'
'Queen Elizabeth's keys.'
'Pass, Queen Elizabeth's keys. All is well.'

The Chief Warder and his escort next meet the main guard, who present arms to them. The Chief Warder raises his bonnet and cries, 'God preserve Queen Elizabeth.' The others reply, 'Amen'. A bugler sounds the Last Post and the keys are lodged with the Resident Governor, as the chief officer of the Tower is called. The Tower is now deemed secure for the night, and only those equipped with the password may come and go.

To see the Tower's other principal ceremony, that of Beating the Bounds, the visitor may have to wait nearly three years. Every third Ascension Day the ancient boundaries of the Tower are proven by a party of boys who tour the grounds and tap the thirty-one Crown Boundary Marks with willow wands. The boys are members of families living in the Tower; the ceremony has its origin in the Middle Ages, when there were few reliable maps, and the physical act of marking the boundaries was thought to carry greater weight.

An odd story surrounds the Tower's ravens. It is said that should they leave, the Tower will fall, and with it the nation. Six ravens are therefore kept, the responsibility of the Raven Master, who ensures the survival of Britain by keeping their wing feathers clipped so that they cannot fly off at will.

right
*Beating the Bounds at the Tower. This ceremony is held once every three years: boys go in procession round the Tower grounds and use willow wands to mark, and symbolically re-establish, the Tower's thirty-one Crown Boundary Marks.*

opposite, above and below left
*Two moments from the nightly Ceremony of the Keys, when the Chief Warder locks the outer gate and those of the Middle and Byward Towers. On his return he and his escort are challenged by a sentry at the Bloody Tower* (above). *After a ritual exchange of words, the Chief Warder raises his bonnet* (below left) *and cries, 'God preserve Queen Elizabeth.'*

opposite, below right
*The Raven Master with one of his fierce charges, survivors from the days when there was a menagerie at the Tower.*

Horses light and heavy –
indispensable to the activities of
ceremonial London.

below left
A troop of the Blues and Royals,
one of the two regiments forming
the Household Cavalry. They ride
black horses.

below right
Trumpeters of the Household
Cavalry; traditionally the
trumpeters are mounted on grey
horses.

bottom
The procession of the annual Lord
Mayor's Show returns from the
Law Courts. The newly elected
Mayor rides in a gilded coach
drawn by six heavy horses and
escorted by a bodyguard of the
Company of Pikemen and
Musketeers.

The Garter ceremony at St George's Chapel, Windsor, held each year to instal new Knights Companion of the Order of the Garter. The Order was founded in 1348 by Edward III. The original garter fell from the leg of the Countess of Salisbury while she was dancing with the King at a ball. The King swooped to pick it up and gallantly declared that he would make it eternally famous.

# Changing the Guard

Two guard-changing ceremonies take place, one involving cavalry regiments, the other the infantry of the Queen's Guard. In the former, the Changing of the Queen's Life Guard at the Horse Guards in Whitehall, the two mounted regiments making up the Household Cavalry – the Life Guards and the Blues and Royals – each perform alternate twenty-four hour guard duty. Their duties include manning the arches and sentry boxes in Whitehall, often a test for both man and horse who must remain unmoving as crowds press closer, cameras click, sugar lumps are waved about and remarks of a sometimes personal nature are heard. The ceremony begins at 11.00, when the new guard arrives at Horse Guards Arch from Knightsbridge Barracks and forms up opposite the old guard. Once installed, the new guard remains on duty until the following day; an inspection on foot takes place at 16.00.

Viewing space at the Horse Guards is severely restricted by the small size of the forecourt, and many visitors prefer to forego the spectacle of the Life Guards' fine black horses in favour of a larger arc of vision at Buckingham Palace. There, from a position along the front railings, one may observe the grander ceremony of the Changing of the Queen's Guard. This usually takes place every other day, and for the most part involves two of the five regiments of the Guards Division – the Grenadier, Coldstream, Scots, Irish and Welsh Guards. All wear a scarlet tunic and bearskin cap or busby, the regiments being differentiated by the grouping of the buttons on their tunics and by plumes of various colours worn in the busby (or no plume at all in the case of the Scots Guards).

The new guard marches into the forecourt at 11.30, preceded by the band that has accompanied it from either Chelsea or Wellington Barracks. The old and new guards face each other across the forecourt and then change about. When the Court is in London, the regiments carry the Queen's Colour, a crimson standard; on other days they carry their regimental colours. At various times, and according to availability, other regiments share duty at the Palace with the Guards.

opposite
*Bandsmen of the Guards Division march away from Buckingham Palace, escorting the old guard back to its barracks after the ceremony of the Changing of the Guard.*

left
*The old and new guard in the forecourt of Buckingham Palace during the ceremony; the nearer men are Scots Guards, distinguishable from other Guards regiments by their buttons, worn in groups of three.*

below
*A sergeant of the Welsh Guards (five buttons) drills his sentries outside Buckingham Palace.*

*Members of the Life Guards Regiment, which with the Blues and Royals forms the Queen's Household Cavalry. The Life Guards are mounted on black horses and wear red tunics and white helmet plumes and carry a white sheepskin on the saddle; the Blues and Royals wear blue tunics and red plumes, with a black sheepskin. When mounted, both regiments wear the Guards helmet and cuirass (front and back plate); these are relics of the days before the tank and rapid-fire weapons, when sabre-swinging heavy cavalrymen (cuirassiers) were a decisive force on the battlefield.*

# Trooping the Colour

Usually it is a hot day; too hot for at least one unfortunate guardsman, who wilts, passes out, and next day finds himself on the front page of his newspaper, stretched out beside his rifle. As a ceremony it has become such a part of London life, and is by its nature such an orderly event, that its news value is measurable only in terms of what may go wrong. Apart from the occasional soldier playing ninepins with himself, little else does. The Trooping of the Queen's Colour, held in honour of the Queen's official birthday, is one of the most tightly organized and executed ceremonies in the calendar. The precision marching, in slow and quick time, of the Guards regiments in the march-past is a model of control and teamwork on an impressively grand scale, showing not a waver in the ranks to the panoramic eyes of the television cameras and the tiers of special guests who fringe the parade ground. Memorable, too, is the review by the Queen, who rides past the ranks of her Foot Guard. Following this tour of inspection, she takes the salute as her Colour is trooped before her; the ceremony is then completed with the combined march-past of all five regiments of Foot Guards.

The Horse Guards Parade, the largest open space of its kind in London, is filled with dense blocks of scarlet and black – the tunics and bearskin caps of the Foot Guards. These are flanked by other scarlets and blacks, the tunics of the Household Cavalrymen mounted on sleek black chargers; the horsemen's plumes of white or red hang from the tops of their bright helmets, the latter gleaming like their cuirasses and ceremonial swords. It is, too, a grand occasion for the military bands who march and counter-march behind their mace-twirling drum-majors, whose gold and scarlet State dress – crowned with a black velvet jockey cap, white high-buttoned gaiters on their legs – suggests it was conceived at some earlier age. Then one remembers that it was the Grenadier Guards who inaugurated military music in Britain, the first regimental band being raised by them in 1685. On such State occasions, the opulence and great depth of British tradition is evident for all to see.

*right*
*The massed bands at the Trooping the Colour ceremony.*

*opposite*
*The Queen inspects the men of her Foot Guard regiments. She then takes the salute as the royal colours are trooped before her. The ceremony closes with a combined march-past.*

*Dawn over the City, from
Waterloo Bridge. Beside the dome
of St Paul's the monolithic hulks
of office blocks stretch away down
river, beyond Southwark Bridge.*

# Along the Thames

To develop a little the line of the poet Edmund Spenser, who in the sixteenth century wrote, 'Sweet Thames run softly, till I end my song': it still runs softly enough but could never be called sweet in any gustatory sense. If its brown-black colour fails to sound sufficient warning we could, but will refrain from recalling the dreadful things that Thames oarsmen say a mere mouthful will do to anyone who falls in. Probably Spenser was using the word 'sweet' in the sense of 'dear' rather than of 'pleasing odour'. Not necessarily though, for the river was still, a century after Spenser, clear enough for noblemen to dive into it from the terraces of their waterside mansions. However, Spenser would probably be cheered to learn that today the river is chemically in better shape than it has been for many years – a fact borne out by the numbers and varieties of fish now to be found, and angled for, in the reaches of Central London, that is, between, roughly, Battersea and Tower Bridges.

More important, perhaps, than its perfume or opacity, the Thames is an invaluable vantage point from which to see London, observing how the great machine works and how it has changed. The river traffic was once brisker: engravings of the Thames around London Bridge tend to depict almost as many craft on the water as buildings on the bank. Traders and ferries plied up, down and across, fetching and delivering at the numerous water-steps and warehouses that line the shores. In the eighteenth century the fare for a boat crossing, anywhere from Vauxhall to Limehouse, was fourpence. In the following century the Thames's function as a main thoroughfare was usurped by the appearance of more and more new road bridges – currently fourteen from Hammersmith to the Tower – and others carrying the railways; by the arrival, too, of buses and underground trains, and the possibilities they offered of rapid conveyance in every direction known to the compass.

In time the riches brought into London arrived less and less by river, and the pickings available to the mudlarks, those Victorian waders, mostly children, who scavenged the shores at low tide, were reduced to lumps of coal or old iron, rope, bones and copper nails. Something of the desolation of a deserted highway now hangs over the Thames and is not dispelled by the odd passing barge or pleasure steamer. For Romantics, seeking a location to sympathize with a mood, this is fine; the river is a constant and varied source. By night the floodlighting of St Paul's, the myriad bulbs on

Chelsea Bridge, contrast with the black liquid ribbon that winds between them. By day there are a hundred vistas to make the spirit soar, from Westminster to the Pool of London, and downstream to Greenwich. In a gentler mood it is pleasant to move upstream, where the river seems narrower, and there imitate the mudlarks, wandering the shore at Strand-on-the-Green or Isleworth; it is calmer here, and a sudden flight of ducks seems almost to bring a whiff of the open countryside.

*Cranes, cargo vessels and tugs in the Pool of London, the name given to the reaches of the Thames below London Bridge, effectively the limit for ocean-going ships; this photograph shows the view looking east from Tower Bridge.*

left

*The 'Prospect of Whitby', an East End riverside pub at Wapping. Many East End pubs put on live music and other entertainments and have a reputation for red-nosed jollity that draws people from the more staid and fashionable districts.*

below

*A panorama of the Thames, dominated by the Victorian Gothic towers of Jones's and Barry's Tower Bridge, built in 1886–94 on gigantic piers. Two 1,000-ton drawbridges are raised to admit tall vessels to the Pool of London, beyond.*

opposite
*The South Bank promenade between Waterloo and Hungerford Bridges, with the Houses of Parliament rising above the latter. On the left are the concrete balconies of a complex that houses the Royal Festival Hall, the Queen Elizabeth Hall, the Purcell Room and the Hayward Gallery.*

left
*The new National Theatre building on the South Bank, opened in 1976.*

below
*The* Discovery, *Captain Scott's Antarctic ship, moored on the Victoria Embankment below Waterloo Bridge.*

above left
*The fumy wastes of Transpontine
London – as natives of smarter
districts affect to call the regions
across the water – here represented
by the chimneys of Battersea
Power Station, seen from behind
railings on the Chelsea bank.*

opposite, below
*A No. 49 bus crosses Battersea Bridge, heading north, above a party of anglers. Thanks to recent efforts, the river is now much cleaner than it used to be, and more varieties of fish have come to live in metropolitan waters.*

above
*A broad sweep of the Thames seen at evening from the entrance to one of the basins at Wapping, in the heart of Dockland. A pleasure steamer plies its evening route between Tower Pier and Greenwich.*

*Outdoor drinkers on a summer's evening at 'The Swan', an old coaching inn on the Bayswater Road. In its early days this was probably the first stopping place west of Tyburn (Marble Arch); in the first decades of the nineteenth century it had a tea garden and a skittles ground.*

# Londoners at Large

What keeps Londoners going is not very different from anywhere else. They shop to feed their bellies with food, their minds with newspapers and books, and for clothes to keep their bodies warm; they go to pubs and theatres, argue and sue each other afterwards. The difference between doing these things in London, rather than in a provincial town, is of style. In London the options are wider: you can buy everything you want in a hypermarket, take it home and lock the door. No trouble. Some Londoners don't like trouble. Generations of living pressed unnaturally close together have tended to accentuate variations of character, producing a breed whose ranks are heightened by compulsive comedians, violent recluses and sharp businessmen. The tendency to be both matey and acid lurks in them all; the decision which to be at any one time can be hard, leading to the long mute periods that some observers have put down to English reserve. This is a great oversimplification. Firstly, Londoners are not to be confused with rural or even other species of urban English. Secondly, as the Creator gave the chameleon his camouflage, so He made the Londoner ambiguous. Thus while he or she, silently strap-hanging on the Underground, may seem to have succumbed to the sub-urban ghosts of seemliness and reserve, the reality may well be different. Unlike the countryman or urban provincial who arrives at work after a brief walk or hermetically sealed car journey, the Londoner must prepare for work in public. In Tube and bus the morning newspaper is absorbed, the first cigarette taken down, reflections cast on what the postman may or may not have brought, and the strategic situation in office or factory assessed for another day's survival and/or advancement. All this goes on against the hissing, thudding, dinging, roaring of the vehicle, and the jockeying and endless side-stepping needed to acquire and maintain a seat.

Why do they do it? Why, because in their sometimes misleadingly grim way they enjoy it. The glamour and the style of it. The chance, for example,

right
*At the sign of the Mona Lisa: the
music man and his parrot, veteran
entertainers both, play for visitors
to the market in Portobello Road,
Notting Hill, at its best and
busiest on Saturdays.*

below
*No strangers to Piccadilly Circus
are this camel-coated coachman
and his elegant black and gold
four-wheeler, waiting for the
traffic lights to change.*

to buy groceries at Harrod's or Fortnum & Mason or Jackson's in Piccadilly. The chance to save up and buy a pair of hand-made shoes or an expensive coat, long admired – a pleasure sharpened, should they work at the particular shop, by the staff discount. The chance to see shows and films when they first appear, and concerts which may not be heard anywhere else. In short, the chance to enjoy the best, as and when it turns up or they want it. And if such considerations should seem unduly shallow or materialistic, then their critic should first sample the trials of obtaining similar benefits outside London;

the experience may send him or her quickly back to town.

This chapter exhibits some of the specialities of London life: the extraordinary markets for antiques, meat and fish (the transfer of the fruit and vegetable market from Covent Garden to a site across the river is still deeply felt and there is no pictorial mention of the new place). Also gladly displayed are the theatres, the street entertainers, some expensive shops and a second-hand bookstore. All are within a few minutes' walk or ride of each other. That is the essence of London.

*The Pearlies, dressed in ornamental costermonger suits covered with mother-of-pearl buttons, as many as twenty or thirty thousand to a single outfit. The Pearly kings and queens of London make public appearances for charity, and hold their own Harvest Festival service at St Martin-in-the-Fields.*

*Reflective contentment, we hope, is registering on the face of this departing customer of Simpson's eighteenth-century chop-house in Ball Court, Cornhill.*

left
*On the floor at Lloyd's, centre of the marine insurance world. Transactions are initiated by the brokers, who walk around and visit the underwriters in their 'boxes'.*

above
*In wig and gown, lawyers pause in Lincoln's Inn Fields, designed in 1618 by Inigo Jones; the largest square in Central London, the old houses surrounding it are mainly occupied by solicitors. At lunchtime, in fine weather, a large male audience is drawn there by the prospect of seeing office girls in shorts dash and pirouette around the netball courts.*

above
*Leather-capped porters and crates of fish at Billingsgate, London's principal fish market. The market is busiest in the early morning, from 05.30; on Sundays it deals only in shellfish.*

right
*Carcasses hang in the great iron arcades of Smithfield meat market. Like Billingsgate, the early morning is the time of greatest activity. Smithfield's connections with livestock go back to the fourteenth century, when the 'Smoothfield' served as a cattle market and tourney ground.*

above left
*A rich display of Fruit & Veg beneath a crown of pineapples and light bulbs in Berwick Street market, Soho.*

left
*The booming antiques trade in the Portobello Road; other antiques markets are at Camden Passage and the New Caledonian in Tower Bridge Road.*

above
*The handbag man in Petticoat Lane (Middlesex Street), perhaps the best known of London's street markets, open only on Sunday mornings. Writing in about 1850, Henry Mayhew described the Sunday markets thus: 'Walnuts, blacking, apples, onions, braces, combs, turnips, herrings, pens, and corn-plaster, are all bellowed out at the same time. Labourers and mechanics, still unshorn and undressed, hang about with their hands in their pockets, some with their pet terriers under their arms. The pavement is green with the refuse leaves of vegetables. . . .' It isn't so very different today.*

*All kinds of places to live. On a barge,* above, *on the Regent's Park Canal, or in one of the elegant houses overlooking it; in one of the small, bow-fronted houses, formerly shops, in Goodwin's Court, off St Martin's Lane, shown* opposite, above; *or,* opposite, below, *protected by a painted dragon in Artesian Road, Notting Hill, not a stone's throw from the bright colours of Portobello Road market.*

right
*Second-hand books in the open air in the Charing Cross Road; this street is more crammed with new and second-hand bookshops than any other in London.*

below
*Buying fish in the grand manner, in Harrod's Food Hall, where an extra pleasure awaits in the shape of the special arrangement of fish on the main slab; a fresh tableau is assembled every morning.*

left
*An auction of Old Master
drawings beneath chandeliers at
Sotheby's in New Bond Street,
one of the world's premier auction
rooms.*

below
*At Lock & Co, the hatters, in
St James's Street. After many
measurements, expertly taken,
some in places where new
customers didn't know they had
measurements, the hat is ready for
trying on.*

*The domes of Shaftesbury Avenue*
*curve uphill to Cambridge Circus.*
*Here are some of the most famous*
*West End theatres – the Apollo,*
*the Globe (not Shakespeare's,*
*that was in Southwark),*
*the Lyric, the Palace, the Queen's –*
*as well as a handful of cinemas.*

top left
*One of the eccentric dancers and street entertainers who have long played to cinema queues on the north side of Leicester Square; his present preoccupation is to encourage a remarkably snake-like brassiere, with at least three cups, to rise from its container.*

top right
*A football fan, in town on Cup Final night, takes the waters in Trafalgar Square.*

above
*Naughty London? A cinema in the Charing Cross Road promises unbounded excitement within. Will they, won't they, take off those little green stickers? Naughty London, unfortunately, is a place of limited delights.*

*The leafy pleasures of Hampstead
Heath, where foxes live and
Londoners may lose themselves
among the thickly wooded vales.*

# Excursions

Windsor and Hampton Court are the attractions most likely to be suggested when a day trip out of town is under consideration. They are described in greater detail on pages 92–95. Beside these two, a royal castle and a royal palace, are many more modest houses, parks and gardens that the visitor may also like to try, perhaps having once sampled the former.

A centre for a tour might be Richmond, a pleasant town on the Thames where the amateur boatman may exercise his skill and picnickers find many pretty spots, not least in Richmond Park (see also Chapter 2). Near by are the Royal Botanic Gardens at Kew: admission to the Gardens costs a healthy 1p, and there are botanic marvels to be observed all the year round in, for instance, the Herbarium, the Rock Garden, the Arboretum and the Aquatic Garden – and superb architecture as well. The famous Palm House by Decimus Burton is an extraordinarily sensuous building, its long curved walls of glass prefiguring Paxton's Crystal Palace. Also at Kew is a 225-foot-high flagstaff made from a Douglas spruce, and Sir William Chambers's Orangery and Pagoda, the latter expressing all its eighteenth-century creator's love of chinoiserie as well as being a landmark for many miles around. More modest is the thatched Queen's Cottage, set in a woodland garden thick-carpeted with bluebells in spring, a favourite with Queen Victoria who asked for it to be preserved in a semi-wild state.

Other famous houses and parks on this western edge of London are Ham House, Ham, built in 1610 and rich in its original furnishings; Osterley House, Osterley, built in about 1575 and remodelled in the latter part of the eighteenth century by the brothers Adam, who decorated it with fine furniture and carpets; and Marble Hill House, Twickenham, a splendid Palladian house set in pleasant parkland that runs down to the towpath. On the London side of Richmond is Chiswick House, a classical villa and park by Lord Burlington and William Kent, and Hogarth's House. The latter was for fifteen years the famous painter's country home, and it contains many of his drawings and engravings. Not to be missed are the splendidly mixed charms of Syon House, Brentford: these include the Jacobean House, with eighteenth-century furniture and interiors by Robert Adam, a large park in which sheep calmly graze . . . and where in one corner the London Transport Collection is housed – a polished and nostalgia-provoking array of old buses, trams, trolleybuses, posters and ephemera. While on a mechanical note, it is worth also mentioning the stream and traction engines now on display at Kew Bridge Pumping Station; among these are the five Cornish beam engines, built between 1820 and 1871 and now restored, that supplied West London with its water until 1944, when they were retired.

Of the other outlying districts there is space to mention just one more – the neighbouring northern suburbs of Hampstead and Highgate, flanked by the magnificent open Heath. Within the Heath is Kenwood House, its grounds the setting in summer for occasional outdoor concerts; while in Keats Grove, Hampstead, is the poet's house, containing a collection of manuscripts, paintings, drawings and relics of Keats and Fanny Brawne, who inspired his greatest love poems.

opposite
*Kew Gardens: beyond the rich beds of tulips is Decimus Burton's Palm House, a triumph in iron and glass, built in 1848. The terrace in front is peopled with the 'Queen's beasts', sculpted for the coronation of Elizabeth II.*

top left
*Elegant seclusion in Pond Square, Highgate, a North London suburb more than usually well provided with good domestic architecture.*

top right
*The curving steps of the grand staircase of the west front of Osterley House, now a National Trust property, built in about 1575 and remodelled in 1761–80 by the brothers Adam.*

above
*Chiswick House, built in 1730 by Lord Burlington and William*

*Kent in a classical style based on the Villa Capra, Vicenza. In the early nineteenth century the Dukes of Devonshire gave lavish dinners here. The park is also open to the public: with its hedges now slightly overgrown, its vistas not always arrow-straight, it is a charming and restful place to walk.*

# Hampton Court

Squattish and turreted, the front façade of Henry VIII's Tudor palace gives a misleadingly modest impression of the splendours lying across the moat and beyond the Great Gatehouse. The Palace was begun in 1514 by Cardinal Wolsey, and the oriel windows of the gatehouse are from his period of occupation, until 1529, when he was obliged to cede the building and its grounds to Henry VIII. That he gave it up seems to have been due to royal envy at the beauty of the new palace rather than as a mark of disfavour. The energetic and uxorious king then launched on a programme of expansion: he built the bridge across the moat and added the Great Hall, noted for its fine hammerbeam roof, and the Chapel. For two centuries Hampton Court was a royal residence, the last monarch to live there being George II.

Inside, the Palace consists of an interlocking set of courts. From the gatehouse the visitor penetrates to Base Court, the largest, in the far wall of which Anne Boleyn's Gateway leads to Clock Court, which takes its name from the astronomical clock there, made for Henry VIII by Nicholas Oursian and which indicates the hour, the month, the phases of the moon and the time of high water at London Bridge. From Clock Court steps lead up to the King's Great Hall, its walls richly hung with tapestries. To the east of the Great Hall is the Watching Chamber, which has a fine plaster ceiling. A colonnade in Clock Court is a later addition, by Wren in 1690; he was also responsible for the large cloistered Fountain Court to the east, through which the formal gardens are reached.

The gardens are dominated by the Long Water, running at right angles away from the east façade, and by the surrounding fan of tree-lined avenues. On the north side is the famous Maze, and to the south are the Privy Garden, with decorative iron gates by Jean Tijou (whose work in St Paul's is mentioned earlier); the Great Vine of 1769, now some seven feet in circumference and still producing a large annual crop of black grapes; and the Pond Garden, a sunken garden laid out by the indefatigable Henry VIII.

opposite
*Wren's east front, seen from across the Long Water. On this side of the Palace formal walks fan out across the Home Park.*

left
*The red brick of Wolsey's Great Gatehouse; a moat runs along the front of the Palace, whose roof-line is continually broken by a profusion of turrets and tall Tudor chimneys.*

below
*The colourful gardens, laid out with a strict eye for symmetry, the sculptured figures and clipped hedges parading in perpetual balance.*

# Windsor Castle

By contrast with Hampton Court, Windsor Castle is still lived in by monarchs: each year members of the Royal Family periodically occupy the Private Apartments in the East Front of the Upper Ward, overlooking the sunken garden. A measure of their love of the Castle is the fact that since 1917 Windsor has been the surname adopted by the Royal Family. George V began this tradition when he abandoned the German family name of Saxe-Coburg-Gotha, and it has been continued by his grand-daughter, the present Queen Elizabeth II.

Like the Tower of London, the Castle is the creation of William the Conqueror, who selected the hill at Windsor as a suitable strategic point from which to defend the western approaches to London. As mentioned in the *Domesday Book* of 1084, the building was then a timber fortress of which no trace survives today – although in layout it may have been similar to the present Castle, with an artificial mound and tower in the centre flanked by upper and lower wards. The stone 'shell-keep' of the Round Tower, with its elongated baileys or walled enclaves running away from the foot of the mound and enclosing the wards, was begun in about 1170. Successive monarchs added walls and towers, the whole being greatly restored in the reigns of George IV and Queen Victoria.

The most striking building within the Castle complex is St George's Chapel, built in 1478–1511, the home of the annual Garter ceremony at which new Knights of the Order are invested (see Chapter 3). It is a splendid example of the Perpendicular style, with superb stained glass and fan-vaulting supported on slender columns. Across the middle of the Chapel runs a tall stone screen in the Gothic style, separating the nave and west end from the chapel choir. In the choir two rows of brilliant standards – the banners of the Knights of the Garter – hang just below the roof; below, the choir stalls are richly carved and date from about 1480. Among the royal personages buried here are Edward IV, Henry VI, Henry VIII, Jane Seymour (the latter's third wife), Charles I, George III, George IV, William IV and George VI (father of the present Queen).

left
*An aerial view of the Castle from the west. In the foreground is St George's Chapel and the lawns of the Lower Ward, and on the crest of the hill rises the moated Round Tower with, beyond it, the Great Quadrangle containing the State apartments.*

below
*The Round Tower from the Thames.*

opposite
*The Queen's Audience Chamber, decorated with tapestries from the Gobelins, Paris, and a ceiling by Verrio exalting Queen Catherine of Braganza.*

# Acknowledgments

Aspect Picture Library, London — 79 *below* (Derek Bayes); 80–81 (Bob Davis)

John Bethell, St Albans — contents spread; 20–21; 22–23; 26 *below*; 33 *below*; 35; 36–37; 46 *below*

British Tourist Authority Photographic Library, London — 14 *above*; 27; 30 *below right*; 31; 38 *below*; 39; 40 *above right*; 45 *above* and *below*; 46 *above*; 51; 55 *below*; 59; 60–61; 68; 79 *above*; 84 *below*; 85 *above* and *below*; 87 *above right*; 90; 91 *above left*

Colorific!, London — 74–75 (B. Angove); 80 *above* (Terence le Goubin); 81 *above* (Penny Tweedie)

Crown copyright — 91 *below*; 93 *below* reproduced with permission of the Controller of Her Majesty's Stationery Office

Daily Telegraph Colour Library, London — 87 *below* (Dmitri Kasterine)

Angelo Hornak, London — 12–13; 21 *above*; 26 *above left* and *above right*; 38 *above*; 69 *above*; 72–73; 93 *above*

Jarrold & Sons, Norwich — 18; 19 *above, below left,* and *below right*; 24 *above* and *below*; 25; 28; 29; 30 *above* and *below left*; 32; 33 *above*; 41 *above* and *below*; 55 *above*; 56; 57 *above, below left* and *below right*; 58 *above left, above right,* and *below*; 61 *above* and *below*; 62; 64; 72 *above*; 94; 95 *above*

A. F. Kersting, London — half-title page; 16–17; 34 *below*; 92; 95 *below*

Denys Lasdun and Partners, London — 71 *above*

National Trust — 91 *above right* (John Bethell)

Spectrum Colour Library, London — preface spread; 14 *below*; 15; 21 *below*; 34 *above left*; 40 *above left*; 42–43; 44; 50; 72 *below*; 76 *above* and *below*; 78; 80 *below*; 81 *below*; 83 *above*; 84 *above*; 86; 87 *above left*

Tony Stone Associates, London — front cover; endpapers; title spread; 34 *above right*; 40 *below*; 47; 48; 52–53; 54–55; 63; 65; 66–67; 68–69; 70; 71 *below*; 77; 82–83; 88–89; back cover

Transworld Feature Syndicate (UK), Sevenoaks — 83 *below* (Tim Graham)

Zoological Society of London — 49